How To Use This Study Guide

This five-lesson study guide corresponds to *"Why Do Bad Things Happen to Good People?" With Rick Renner* (Renner TV). Each lesson in this study guide covers a topic that is addressed during the program series, with questions and references supplied to draw you deeper into your own private study of the Scriptures on this subject.

To derive the most benefit from this study guide, consider the following:

First, watch or listen to the program prior to working through the corresponding lesson in this guide. (Programs can also be viewed at **renner.org** by clicking on the Media/Archives links or on our Renner Ministries YouTube channel.)

Second, take the time to look up the scriptures included in each lesson. Prayerfully consider their application to your own life.

Third, use a journal or notebook to make note of your answers to each lesson's Study Questions and Practical Application challenges.

Fourth, invest specific time in prayer and in the Word of God to consult with the Holy Spirit. Write down the scriptures or insights He reveals to you.

Finally, take action! Whatever the Lord tells you to do according to His Word, do it.

For added insights on this subject, it is recommended that you obtain Rick's book ***Build Your Foundation: Six Must-Have Beliefs for Constructing an Unshakable Life***. You may also select from Rick's other available resources by placing your order at **renner.org** or by calling 1-800-742-5593.

LESSON 1

TOPIC

The Biggest Culprit — The Curse Opened the Door to Bad Things

SCRIPTURES

1. **Genesis 3:17,18** — And unto Adam he [God] said, Because thou hast hearkened unto the voice of thy wife, and hast eaten of the tree, of which I commanded thee, saying, Thou shalt not eat of it: cursed is the ground for thy sake.... Thorns also and thistles shall it bring forth to thee; and thou shalt eat the herb of the field.
2. **Exodus 20:7** — Thou shalt not take the name of the Lord thy God in vain; for the Lord will not hold him guiltless that taketh his name in vain.
3. **Romans 5:12** — Wherefore, as by one man sin entered into the world, and death by sin; and so death passed upon all men....
4. **Romans 5:15** — But not as the offence, so also is the free gift. For if through the offence of one many be dead, much more the grace of God, and the gift by grace, which is by one man, Jesus Christ, hath abounded unto many.
5. **Romans 5:17** — For if by one man's offence death reigned by one; much more they which receive abundance of grace and of the gift of righteousness shall reign in life by one, Jesus Christ.
6. **Romans 5:21** — That as sin hath reigned unto death, even so might grace reign through righteousness unto eternal life by Jesus Christ our Lord.
7. **1 John 5:4** — For whatsoever is born of God overcometh the world: and this is the victory that overcometh the world, even our faith.

HEBREW WORDS

1. "cursed" — ררא (*arar*): to bitterly and horribly curse
2. "ground" — המדא (*adamah*): everything related to the earth-realm
3. "for thy sake" — רובע (*abur*): on account of you, because of you

A Note From Rick Renner

I am on a personal quest to see a "revival of the Bible" so people can establish their lives on a firm foundation that will stand strong and endure the test as end-time storm winds begin to intensify.

In order to experience a revival of the Bible in your personal life, it is important to take time each day to read, receive, and apply its truths to your life. James tells us that if we will continue in the perfect law of liberty — refusing to be forgetful hearers, but determined to be doers — we will be blessed in our ways. As you watch or listen to the programs in this series and work through this corresponding study guide, I trust you will search the Scriptures and allow the Holy Spirit to help you hear something new from God's Word that applies specifically to your life. I encourage you to be a doer of the Word He reveals to you. Whatever the cost, I assure you — it will be worth it.

> Thy words were found, and I did eat them;
> and thy word was unto me the joy and rejoicing of mine heart:
> for I am called by thy name, O Lord God of hosts.
> —Jeremiah 15:16

Your brother and friend in Jesus Christ,

Rick Renner

Unless otherwise indicated, all scripture quotations are taken from the *King James Version* of the Bible.

Scripture quotations marked (*MSG*) are taken from *The Message*, copyright © 1993, 2002, 2018 by Eugene H. Peterson. Used by permission of NavPress. All rights reserved. Represented by Tyndale House Publishers, Inc.

Scripture quotations marked (*NKJV*) are taken from the *New King James Version*®. Copyright © 1982 by Thomas Nelson. Used by permission. All rights reserved.

Scripture quotations marked (*NLT*) are taken from the Holy Bible, *New Living Translation*, copyright © 1996, 2004, 2015 by Tyndale House Foundation. Used by permission of Tyndale House Publishers, Inc., Carol Stream, Illinois 60188. All rights reserved.

Why Do Bad Things Happen to Good People?

Copyright © 2025 by Rick Renner
1814 W. Tacoma St.
Broken Arrow, OK 74012-1406

Published by Rick Renner Ministries
www.renner.org

ISBN 13: 978-1-6675-1155-9

ISBN 13 eBook: 978-1-6675-1156-6

All rights reserved. No portion of this book may be reproduced or transmitted in any form or by any means — electronic, mechanical, photocopy, recording, scanning, or other — except for brief quotations in critical reviews or articles, without the prior written permission of the Publisher.

4. "thorns" — קוֹץ (*qots*): thorns or thornbushes; something dangerous, hurtful, or prickly; hurtful situations; used figuratively to describe enemies
5. "thistles" — דַּרְדַּר (*dardar*): thistles; something running freely or out of control
6. "herb" — עֵשֶׂב (*eseb*): grass or herbs; something very different from what was grown in the garden in Eden
7. "of the field" — הַשָּׂדֶה (*sadeh*): country, ground, wild land, or battlefield

GREEK WORDS

1. "wherefore" — Διὰ τοῦτο (*dia touto*): on account of this; as a result of this; consequently
2. "world" — κόσμος (*kosmos*): the world; depicts anything fashioned or ordered; denotes systems and institutions in society, such as fashion, education, or entertainment; everything related to the world, including nature and human systems
3. "death" — θάνατος (*thanatos*): death, either physical or spiritual; a death sentence; but here used with a definite article meaning THE death, referring to an all-pervasive death
4. "offense" — παράπτωμα (*paraptoma*): lapse; violation; a known violation
5. "death" — θάνατος (*thanatos*): death, either physical or spiritual; a death sentence
6. "reigned" — βασιλεύω (*basileuo*): to reign; to reign like a king; to reign as king; to exercise kingly authority
7. "reign" — βασιλεύω (*basileuo*): to reign; to reign like a king; to reign as king; to exercise kingly authority
8. "overcometh" — νικάω (*nikao*): to conquer; to conquest; to master; to overcome; to prevail; to subdue; to have victory
9. "victory" — νίκη (*nike*): conquest; mastery; victory
10. "that overcometh" — νικήσασα (*nikesasa*): better or having overcome
11. "world" — κόσμος (*kosmos*): the world; depicts anything fashioned or ordered; denotes systems and institutions in society, such as fashion, education, or entertainment; everything related to the world, including nature and human systems

SYNOPSIS

The five lessons in this study titled *Why Do Bad Things Happen to Good People* will focus on the following topics:

- The Biggest Culprit — The Curse Opened the Door to Bad Things
- Lack of Knowledge Opens the Door to Bad Things
- Disobedience Opens the Door to Bad Things
- Stupidity Opens the Door to Bad Things
- Devilish Attacks Open the Door to Bad Things

Have you ever wondered why bad things happen to good people? Or why calamities and tragedies happen for *any* reason? Indeed, dealing with difficulties is not something any of us desire, yet it is an inescapable part of the human experience. These five lessons will help open your eyes to some of the major causes of the problems we face, starting with the biggest culprit — the fall of man.

The emphasis of this lesson:

The first and primary reason bad things happen to good people is because of Adam and Eve's sin. Their disobedience to God's Word opened the door to death and brought a curse upon everything and everyone on the earth. But even though death has reigned since the Fall, through the Cross and resurrection of Jesus, we have a faith available for us to walk in that overcomes the curse.

Man's Disobedience Brought a Curse Upon the Earth

The book of Genesis is the book of beginnings — it gives the account of Creation and the origin of mankind. After God created the heavens and the earth and everything in them, He then created Adam and Eve and placed them in the Garden of Eden. It was the ideal, perfect environment — absent of sin, sickness, strife, difficulties, and death. Adam and Eve walked in personal fellowship with the Father and experienced a fullness of life like no one else.

Then tragedy struck...Eve yielded to the deception of the enemy and ate of the forbidden fruit and convinced Adam to partake of it as well. In that moment, everything changed. Their disobedience brought a curse upon them and everything on the earth. We read about this event in Genesis 3:17, which says:

> And unto Adam he [God] said, Because thou hast hearkened unto the voice of thy wife, and hast eaten of the tree, of which I commanded thee, saying, Thou shalt not eat of it: cursed is the ground for thy sake....

Many have read this verse and thought that it says God cursed the ground, but that is not what it says. The ground came under a curse because of mankind's disobedience. When Adam and Eve sinned, they opened a spiritual door to the devil and to death, allowing them to enter and wreak havoc on the planet. Thus, the earth is cursed as a result of man's actions.

Taking a closer look at this verse, the Hebrew word for "cursed" is *arar*, which means *to bitterly and horribly curse*. God's will was for mankind to live in a beautiful, perfect environment, but because of Adam and Eve's disobedience, the earth became *bitterly and horribly cursed*.

Specifically, the Bible says, "...Cursed is the ground for thy sake..." (Genesis 3:17). The word "ground" in Hebrew is *adamah*, and it describes *everything related to the earth-realm*. And the phrase "for thy sake" — the Hebrew word *abur* — means *on account of you* or *because of what you have done*. Thus, it was Adam and Eve's disobedient actions that opened the door for death and the devil to come raging into everything related to the earth-realm.

'Thorns and Thistles' Are a Result of the Fall

What else resulted from mankind's disobedience? Genesis 3:18 says, "Thorns also and thistles shall it bring forth to thee; and thou shalt eat the herb of the field." There are several key words in this verse, including the word "thorns." This is the Hebrew word *qots*, which describes *thorns or thornbushes*. It is *something dangerous*, *hurtful*, or *prickly*.

The next important word we see is "thistles," which is *dardar* in Hebrew, and it describes *thistles* or *something running freely or out of control*. The moment Adam and Eve sinned, Eden — which literally means *pleasure and delight* — became a place where there were dangerous and hurtful things. What was once well-managed and under control in a place of peace and safety began to unravel out of control in an environment that suddenly became harmful to them.

God told Adam that he would "...eat the herb of the field" (Genesis 3:18). The Hebrew word for "herb" is *eseb*, which means *grass or herbs*. It was something very different from what was grown in the Garden in Eden. We know this because of the phrase "of the field," a translation of the Hebrew word *sadeh*, which means *country, ground, wild land,* or *battlefield*.

Once Adam and Eve sinned, they opened the door to the devil and death and all of its consequences began to invade. Suddenly, earth went from being a beautiful, peaceful paradise to a wild land or battlefield. Again, it was the effect of mankind's actions that brought about this curse — it was *not* God's doing.

This was the very first time thorns and thistles began to appear on the planet. Before the curse, roses had no thorns, but after the fall of man, suddenly those beautiful things that God created had harm and death attached to them. The world became a thorny, hurtful, dangerous place where people could be hurt and death began to rule as king. Today the curse manifests itself in many forms, including sickness, disease, pestilence, strife, and murder.

Taking the Lord's Name in Vain Is Damaging To His Reputation

With the arrival of the curse also came such things as earthquakes, famines, hurricanes, and tornados. Although insurance companies call these events "acts of God," nothing could be further from the truth.

Sadly, God gets blamed for many tragic happenings that have nothing to do with Him. He is not to blame for what resulted from man's sin and shame. These troublesome things are a direct result of the curse that is working in the earth.

Not long after God delivered the nation of Israel from Egyptian bondage, He gave them the Ten Commandments, which are recorded in Exodus 20. In the third commandment God said, "Thou shalt not take the name of the Lord thy God in vain; for the Lord will not hold him guiltless that taketh his name in vain" (Exodus 20:7).

Now most people think taking the name of the Lord in vain means to use the Lord's name in the context of curse words, and while it certainly can mean that, there is more to it. According to Rabbi Telushkin, a very respected Jewish leader:

...[This verse] makes it clear why God won't forgive the violation of this commandment. It is the only one of the Ten Commandments which turns God into a victim. A person who commits murder, steals, or swears a false oath discredits himself or herself, but a person who does a murderous or odious act in God's name alienates people from God as well. Thus, God suffers from the acts of those who do evil in His name
— Joseph Telushkin
The Book of Jewish Values

When God is blamed for things He didn't do, His reputation is injured. Think of how many people have ill feelings toward God because someone told them God was behind a hurricane, a tornado, or some other evil catastrophe. The fact is God didn't send any of those things, which we will see clearly in our next lesson.

When we ascribe or attribute hurtful, damaging activity and events to the hand of God, we're using the name of the Lord in vain. We're blaming Him for what He did *not* do, and consequently, we're breaking the third commandment.

Man's Sin Opened the Door for Death To Invade the World

Catastrophes and calamities are all the result of Adam and Eve's original sin. Their disobedience caused the curse to come upon the earth and opened the door to death in all its forms, and the effects have been running wild on the planet ever since. This truth is made quite clear in Romans 5:12, which says:

> **Wherefore, as by one man sin entered into the world, and death by sin; and so death passed upon all men....**

Notice the opening word "wherefore." It is a translation of the Greek words *dia touto*, which means *on account of this*, *as a result of this*, or *consequently*. It was *on the account of* or *as a result of* what Adam did that "...sin entered into the world, and death by sin...."

The word "world" is also important. It is the Greek word *kosmos*, which describes *the world* and depicts *anything fashioned or ordered*. Here it denotes systems and institutions in society, such as fashion, education, or entertainment. Moreover, the word *kosmos* refers to *everything related to the world*, including *nature* and *human systems*.

Here we find that when Adam and Eve disobeyed God, sin entered every system in the world, including nature, human institutions, and all aspects of the human race. And with sin came "death." This is the Greek word *thanatos*, and it depicts *death, either physical or spiritual*. It is also the word for *a death sentence*. In Romans 5:12, it is used with a definite article meaning THE death, referring to *an all-pervasive death*.

Hence, when Adam disobeyed, death came rushing into the world and passed upon all men.

Death Has 'Reigned' on Earth Since Adam Sinned

This truth continues to unfold just a few verses later in Romans 5:17, where the apostle Paul wrote:

> **For if by one man's offence death reigned by one; much more they which receive abundance of grace and of the gift of righteousness shall reign in life by one, Jesus Christ.**

Notice the word "offense." It is the Greek word *paraptoma*, which describes *a lapse* or *a known violation*. When Adam reached out and ate of the fruit God told him not to eat, it was a known violation. He knew what he was doing was wrong, and his actions opened the door for death to rush into the world.

Here again, we see the word "death," the Greek word *thanatos*, which describes *death, either physical or spiritual*, or again, *a death sentence*. Thus, as a result of one man's known violation, a death sentence rushed in upon all humanity and all areas of the world and its systems. The original Greek text of Romans 5:17 essentially says, "Because of one…," "On the account of one…," or "Through the actions of one, death *reigned*."

That word "reigned" in Greek is *basileuo*, and it means *to reign, to reign like a king, to reign as king*, or *to exercise kingly authority*. Through Adam and Eve's disobedience, death began to exercise kingly authority on planet Earth and over mankind. The results of its reign are seen in all kinds of sickness and disease as well as strife, wars, murders, hurricanes, earthquakes, tsunamis, and the like. None of these occurred until death took its seat on the throne and began to reign on the earth.

We see this same truth echoed just four verses later, where Paul says, "That as sin hath reigned unto death…" (Romans 5:21). Again, we see the word "reigned," the Greek word *basileuo*, and it means *to reign, to reign like a king, to reign as king,* or *to exercise kingly authority*. The fact that this is repeated over and over in the same chapter emphasizes that when Adam and Eve sinned, they opened the door to death, and it came rushing in and began ruling like a king on the earth, producing horrible effects.

God's Grace Has Dethroned the Authority of Death in Our Lives

Thank God, He did not leave us in that horrible condition. Instead, He sent His only Son, Jesus, to reverse the curse! We see this truth proclaimed multiple times throughout the New Testament, including in the book of Romans, which says:

> **…Much more they which receive abundance of grace and of the gift of righteousness shall reign in life by one, Jesus Christ…. Even so might grace reign through righteousness unto eternal life by Jesus Christ our Lord.**
> **— Romans 5:17,21**

These passages declare that when we receive the abundant grace of God and righteousness through Jesus, we are placed *in Christ*, and the authority of death is dethroned in our lives! Instead of death reigning, the Bible says we "…shall reign in life by one, Jesus Christ" (Romans 5:17). Interestingly, that word "reign" is the same Greek word *basileuo*, which means in Christ, we are meant to *reign like kings* in His righteousness and *exercise kingly authority* in this life and all the way into eternity.

Of course, ultimately, we know that in the resurrection, death will have no grip on us. But what Jesus accomplished through His death on the Cross and His resurrection from the dead, also affects us here and now. He dethroned the rule of death for those who call Him the Lord of their life, which means we no longer have to live with the effects of the curse that Adam's sin brought into the world.

If we will use the name of Jesus, the Word of God, and the authority that He has given us, we can dethrone all the effects of the curse in our lives, including sickness, disease, strife, poverty, and all the things God never intended for us to have to deal with in our lives.

Through Christ, You Have a Faith That Overcomes the World

Friend, through salvation in Jesus Christ, you have been given a faith that overcomes! And that faith is even able to overcome the effects of the curse. The apostle John makes this clear in his first epistle, where he writes:

> **For whatsoever is born of God overcometh the world: and this is the victory that overcometh the world, even our faith.**
> — 1 John 5:4

Are you a born-again child of God? Then this verse is written to you! Through Christ, you have the authority to overcome the world, and that word "overcometh" is the Greek word *nikao*, which means *to conquer, to conquest, to master, to overcome, to prevail, to subdue,* and ultimately *to have victory.* When we insert the meaning of this word into First John 5:4, we could translate the first part:

> **For whatsoever is born of God** *conquers, conquests, masters, prevails over, subdues,* **and ultimately** *has victory over* **the world....**

The word "world" here is the Greek word *kosmos*, the same term used in Romans 5:17 to inform us that the curse brought on by man's sin affected the entire world and all of its systems. But in First John 5:4, the word *kosmos* is used to describe what we as believers are empowered to overcome — *the world*. Again, this depicts *anything fashioned or ordered* and denotes *systems and institutions in society, such as fashion, education, or entertainment.* It is everything related to the world, including nature and human systems. So those of us who are born of God have the authority through Christ to conquer, master, prevail over, and subdue every force working against us, including the curse brought on by man's disobedience.

John goes on to say, "...This is the victory that overcometh the world, even our faith." The word "victory" here is the Greek word *nike*, meaning *conquest, mastery,* or *victory*. The victory or the mastery that overcomes the world is our *faith*. The phrase "that overcometh" is a translation of the Greek word *nikesasa*. It is past tense, so a better translation would be "...having overcome the world."

The word "world" is again the Greek word *kosmos*, which describes *the world* and depicts *anything fashioned or ordered.* Thus, our faith in Christ, in His Word, and in His name is the mastery with which we overcome all the systems and institutions in society. We have victory over everything related to the world, including nature and human systems.

Jesus Restored What Was Lost Through the Fall

So through Adam and Eve's disobedience, a door was opened to the devil and all the effects of death came rushing into the planet. Suddenly, death began to rule and reign and produce thorns and thistles — dangerous and hurtful situations began to wreak havoc on the planet, causing out-of-control circumstances.

Sickness, disease, war, pestilence, climate problems, earthquakes, tornadoes, hurricanes, and the like were not designed or produced by God. They are all the byproduct of the curse, which has been ruling and reigning like a king on the earth since the fall of man.

But for those of us who call Jesus our Lord, the authority of death has been dethroned, decommissioned in our lives! Through faith in His finished work on the Cross, we are now living under God's blessing, and we have the authority to return to a life that is free from the effects of the curse. Jesus restored to us what was lost through the fall of man and, in fact, we are designed by God to reign in life as kings through Christ Jesus — both now and in eternity!

According to First John 5:4, we have a faith that has the authority to master everything in this world. As we feed our soul and spirit the Word of God, operate according to its directives, and use the name of Jesus that has been given to us, we can override everything in the world's system that is coming against those of us in the Kingdom of God. Thus, we can even override the effects of the curse and live in peace, healed and whole.

In our next lesson, we are going to examine how a lack of knowledge can also be a door-opener to problems in our lives.

STUDY QUESTIONS

Study to shew thyself approved unto God, a workman that needeth not to be ashamed, rightly dividing the word of truth.
— 2 Timothy 2:15

1. What is your reaction to hearing the original Hebrew meaning of Genesis 3:17,18? Prior to this lesson, what was your perception of how the earth was cursed and the meaning of "thorns and thistles"? How has your understanding of mankind's sin and our fall from grace increased through this teaching?
2. Take time to carefully read and compare Romans 5:12-20 and First Corinthians 15:20-23; 45-49. What is the Holy Spirit showing you about how sin and death entered through Adam? What is He revealing about how righteousness and grace entered through Jesus? Which person's actions were more powerful? What else are you seeing and learning in these amazing passages?

PRACTICAL APPLICATION

> But be ye doers of the word, and not hearers only, deceiving your own selves.
> —James 1:22

1. Although taking the name of the Lord in vain can mean using His name in the context of curse words, it can also mean accrediting hurtful, damaging activity and events to the hand of God. How does this revelation change the way you view this third commandment? Have you been unknowingly guilty of doing this in the past?
2. Have you ever been around people who blamed God for things He didn't do? Have others ever told you that He was behind a hurricane, a tornado, or some other evil catastrophe? If so, how did their words affect God's reputation in your mind? Do you still have ill feelings toward Him as a result? If so, pray and release your hurt and misunderstanding to the Father and ask Him to forgive you and give you an accurate revelation of who He truly is.

LESSON 2

TOPIC
Lack of Knowledge Opens the Door to Bad Things

SCRIPTURES
1. **Hosea 4:6** — My people are destroyed for lack of knowledge....
2. **James 1:13** — Let no man say when he is tempted, I am tempted of God: for God cannot be tempted with evil, neither tempteth he any man.
3. **James 1:17** — Every good gift and every perfect gift is from above, and cometh down from the Father of lights, with whom is no variableness, neither shadow of turning.

HEBREW WORDS
1. "destroyed" — הָמַד (*damah*): to cease, to cause to cease, to cut off, to destroy, to perish, to be silenced, to be undone, to be brought to destruction, or to be brought to ruin
2. "knowledge" — תַּעַד (*daath*): knowledge, perception, prophetic knowledge, or truth; pictures one who is ignorant, unaware, or unknowledgeable

SYNOPSIS
In Lesson 1, we learned that the main reason bad things happen in this life is because of the curse that came upon the earth due to Adam and Eve's sin. Prior to their disobedience to God's Word, the world was a very different place, one of peace and safety. But after they sinned, thorns and thistles were produced, bringing dangerous and hurtful situations. Even worse, death came raging into the world and began to reign and exercise kingly authority over everything and everyone on the planet and had the absolute right to do so — until the death and resurrection of Christ.

The great news is that for all of us who put our faith in Jesus and make Him Lord of our life, everything has changed. The authority of death has been removed from our lives, and through Christ, we can rule and reign in righteousness. The Cross and the resurrection have put us in a position where, rather than being sick, we can be healed and made whole; rather than being poor, we can be abundantly blessed; rather than walking in strife, we can walk in peace.

Jesus' death and resurrection gives us the authority to live a life more like what God originally intended. First John 5:4 declares that we have a faith that overcomes the world. That is, our faith in Christ and His Word has the authority to override everything that's working against us in the world's systems, including the effects of the curse.

The emphasis of this lesson:

Another reason problems often plague our lives is a lack of knowledge. Some believers live impoverished, sick, and brokenhearted because they don't know the truth of God's Word, which says it is never His will or His nature to send anything evil or miserable into anyone's life. Instead, He is habitually sending us good and profitable gifts that cause us to mature.

What Does It Mean To Be 'Destroyed for Lack of Knowledge'?

In addition to the curse brought upon mankind due to sin, another reason bad things happen to good people — and really, to all people — is a lack of knowledge. God makes this truth crystal clear in Hosea 4:6 where He says, "My people are destroyed for lack of knowledge…."

The Hebrew word for "destroyed" is *damah*, and it means *to cease, to cause to cease*, or *to cut off*. Likewise, it also means *to destroy, to perish, to be silenced, to be undone, to be brought to destruction*, or *to be brought to ruin*. When we take these meanings and insert them into Hosea 4:6, we could translate it as follows:

- My people *cease*, are *caused to cease*, and *are cut off* for a lack of knowledge….

- My people *are destroyed, they perish, they're silenced*, and *they're undone* for a lack of knowledge….

- My people *are brought to destruction* and *brought to ruin* for a lack of knowledge….

The word "knowledge" here is the Hebrew word *daath*, and it describes *knowledge, perception, prophetic knowledge*, or *truth*. Someone with a *lack of knowledge* pictures *one who is ignorant, unaware*, or *unknowledgeable*. Hence, those that are ignorant or unaware of God's truth are precariously predisposed to problems.

Many Believers Live Impoverished Because They Don't Know God Wants Them To Flourish

To help us grasp the devastating effects of a lack of knowledge, Rick shared an example in the program from his own life. Many years ago, he and his wife, Denise, wrongly believed that being poor was their lot in life. Consequently, they found themselves in such a deplorable situation that Rick wrote about it and even included photos of where they lived in their autobiography titled *Unlikely*.

At that time, they had one son, Paul, and were living in a derelict house with barely enough money to pay their bills and buy food. Because they lacked the knowledge of God's Word, they erroneously thought it was God's will for them to live a life of poverty.

Rick said, "During that time, my sister, Ronda, got a new dress, and when Denise and I saw her walking around in it, we thought she was being carnal (fleshly) because she was enjoying material possessions. We, on the other hand, were holy because we were living a life of poverty in a dilapidated house. But the fact is that we were ignorant."

The situation was so bad that on the weekends Rick and Denise would call their friends, who were also poor, and see what kind of leftovers they had in their refrigerators. After conferring with one another, everyone would bring their scraps together and make a mutual meal so that they would all have something to eat.

In their minds, they really believed they were "suffering for Jesus," and being dirt-poor was simply their burden to bear. For some reason they thought that living in poverty was bringing God glory. The truth is, the way they were living was a horrible testimony of who God really was.

In Lesson 1, we saw that taking the Lord's name in vain — which is what we are commanded *not* to do in Exodus 20:7 — includes saying that God is responsible for something He has nothing to do with. When Rick and Denise claimed that it was God's will for them to live in poverty, that is exactly what they were doing. They were accrediting Him with something He had never said. The reason for their deplorable situation was rooted in their not knowing the truth of God's Word.

The first thing the Bible states about Jesus' ministry is that God had anointed Him "…to preach the gospel to the poor…" (Luke 4:18). This lets us know that the Gospel is an economic gamechanger. God doesn't want anyone poor and living in poverty. He sent Jesus that we might have life more abundantly (*see* John 10:10). Those who are ignorant of this truth or choose to believe otherwise will receive what they believe.

Many Believers Live With Sickness Because They Don't Know God Wants Them To Be Healed

What about sickness? Is it God's will for people to be sick at times? Think about it — does that bring Him glory? There are quite a few people who live their lives with this kind of thinking. In fact, there are entire church denominations that believe healing ended when the apostles passed away. You may be attending one of those types of churches.

Rick shared how the church he was a part of during his formative years believed that God was sovereign and that everything that happens in our lives ultimately comes from Him — including sickness. Here again is another example of taking God's name in vain — blaming Him for something He has nothing to do with.

The fact is that most people get sick simply because of the curse that has been working in the earth since Adam and Eve's fall. That is the main culprit for problems in our lives. There were no forms of sickness or disease before the curse came on the world, and we are still living under the effects of that curse today.

So ever since then, the devil and his demons have worked tirelessly to inflict people with one sickness or another, and many believers who are ignorant of the truth simply pray for God's grace to grin and bear it and "glorify Him in their suffering."

The truth is that God desires for you to "…prosper in all things and *be in health*, just as your soul prospers" (3 John 2 *NKJV*). And according to First John 5:4, our faith has the ability to override and master anything that comes against us, which includes sickness. Believers who live with the effects of sickness do so because they don't understand or have knowledge of the truth, and it's their lack of knowledge in this area that is causing their bodies to be destroyed and brought to ruin concerning their health.

Many Believers Live Emotionally Wounded Because They Don't Know Healing the Brokenhearted Is God's Will

How about relationships? Is it God's will that we experience broken marriages and friendships and try to make it through life with a broken heart that's been beaten down by others? There are some people who wear the wounds from past relationships like a badge of courage, believing that holding onto such things and living in such dysfunction somehow brings God glory.

The truth is that one of the main purposes of Jesus' ministry was "to heal the brokenhearted" (*see* Luke 4:18). The word "brokenhearted" in the original Greek language describes people who have been fractured by bad relationships, so much so that they feel like they've been stomped on by others.

If that is you, rather than just struggle emotionally for the rest of your life, know that God wants you to be healed and completely restored to wholeness. Don't believe for one more minute that being brokenhearted is your God-appointed lot in life. That is a lie. Jesus said, "…I am come that they might have life, and that they might have it more abundantly" (John 10:10). And that includes a life of abundance in your relationships.

When We Go Through Crushing Times, God Is Not the One Behind It

James, the half-brother of Jesus, specifically addressed the issue of blaming God for our problems. When he wrote his letter, he was addressing Jewish believers who had been experiencing great hardship, and they were blaming God for what they were going through.

Writing under the inspiration of the Holy Spirit, James wrote:

> **Let no man say when he is tempted, I am tempted of God: for God cannot be tempted with evil, neither tempteth he any man.**
> **—James 1:13**

There are several important words in this passage that we need to understand. For starters, when James said, "Let no man say," it is a very strong prohibition in Greek, which would be better translated, "Stop it! And stop it now! I emphatically want you to stop saying...."

What were James' readers saying? They were claiming that they were being "tempted of God." The word "tempted" here is a Greek word that basically means *to be crushed*, *devastated*, or *destroyed*. Again, these believers were going through extremely tough situations.

When we insert the original meaning of these words into the verse, we could translate the first part of James 1:13, "Stop it, and stop it now! I want you to stop saying when you are being crushed and destroyed, 'I'm being crushed and destroyed of God'...."

What's interesting is that even the tiny word "of" is important. Rather than use the Greek word *hupo*, which means *directly from*, James chose the Greek word *apo*, which means *remotely* or to do something *from a distance*. What does the use of this word tell us?

Well, rather than say, "God Himself is directly behind and personally responsible for these crushing and devastating problems we're experiencing," the believers James was writing to were basically saying, "We know that God is not *personally* crushing us or causing all this misery in our lives. But He is sovereign, and if He wanted to stop it, He could have. Therefore, since He didn't stop it even from a faraway distance (*apo*), He is allowing all these crushing things to come into our lives. It must be His permissive will to allow us to experience all these devastating trials."

When James heard that the believers were saying such things, he said, "Stop talking like that and stop it now! How dare you allege that God is remotely giving permission for the problems you're facing." James then added, "...For God cannot be tempted with evil, neither tempteth he any man" (James 1:13).

In other words, it is never the will of God nor the nature of God to give anything miserable or anything catastrophic to anyone. God cannot be tempted with evil because there is absolutely no evil within Him, so He doesn't have any of that to give to anyone else.

What God Gives and What He Never Gives

It is vital for us to be able to recognize what *is* and what *is not* from God. James helps us better understand the difference by adding these words just four verses later: "Every good gift and every perfect gift is from above, and cometh down from the Father of lights, with whom is no variableness, neither shadow of turning" (James 1:17).

God *never* gives us crushing or devastating things. As we just read in James 1:13, He cannot bring evil into our lives because there is no evil in Him. Instead, God always gives "every good and perfect gift…" (James 1:17). The word "every" is all-encompassing and means *absolutely every* good gift, and the word "gift" depicts *the habitual giving of God*. Rather than a one-time gift, God is giving to us all the time, and the gifts He gives are always *good*. The word "good" here is the Greek word *agathos*, which describes *something beneficial or advantageous*.

When we combine the meaning of all these words together, we learn that every time God gives us something — which is continually — everything He gives us is good, advantageous, beneficial, and profitable. God doesn't have any evil in Him. Therefore, He has nothing evil or crushing to give us.

God *only* gives good and perfect gifts! According to Scripture, everything that comes from God is *good*, *advantageous*, *beneficial*, and *profitable* for you. He gives "gifts," which in the original Greek text describes *the habitual giving of God*, and what God always, always, *always* gives is *good*.

In addition to every good gift, James added every perfect gift. The word "perfect" is a form of the Greek word *teleos*, which describes *something that is completing or maturing*. Moreover, *teleos* was also the word that was used to describe a student who graduated and moved upward from one level into the next. Hence, it indicates *upward mobility* or *upward movement*.

When something is from God, it will always bring completion to your life. What He gives will never take you down but will always result in upward mobility. His gifts cause you to advance and rise higher in life. If you're experiencing anything that's not beneficial, not profitable, or that's taking you down, it's *not* from God. According to James 1:17, it fails the test.

Are you beginning to see how important it is for you to have knowledge of God's Word and know who He is? People are destroyed when they lack knowledge of the truth and it opens the door for problems and calamities to come into their life. If a person believes those things are sent by God, then they will continue to open their life to receive them, and the devil will keep sending them one bad thing after another.

God Showers Us With Gifts That Are Overwhelmingly Good

It is important to note that the wording James used is comparative language. For example, he wrote, "Every good gift and every perfect gift is *from above…*" (James 1:17). Here, James is indirectly comparing the gifts that come *from above* with the things that come *from below* — earthly things that are a result of the curse or are produced by the enemy. What comes from God above is always good, and the implication is that what comes from below — from the world and the enemy — is always bad.

Notice also that James said the gifts from above "…cometh down from the Father of lights…" (James 1:17). The words "cometh down" are a translation of the Greek word *katabaino*, a compound of the words *kata* and *baino*. The word *kata* describes *something dominating, subjugating*, and *conquering*, and the word *baino* means *to come down*. When these words are combined to form *katabaino*, it describes *something that is coming down so hard, heavy, and dominating* that it has an overpowering effect on the recipient.

What's interesting is that this word *katabaino* is the same term that was used by the ancient Greeks to describe a downpour or a thunderstorm. If you've ever been in a downpour while driving your car, you know that the rain comes down so heavy sometimes you can't see the road very well. In fact, it is so subjugating and dominating that you may need to pull over and stop. That is the word James used here to describe the good and perfect gifts that come from God, which means when God showers us with His gifts, they have a dominating and subjugating effect on our life, and they are coming down on us all the time.

Now you may be thinking, *Well, why am I not being hit by any of these gifts?* If you wrongly believe that God is behind all the difficulties in your life, that is more than likely the reason you are not experiencing His fullness in your life. Because of your lack of knowledge concerning what God gives,

Satan keeps sending you one problem after another, trying to make your life miserable so you get more and more angry with God who is not the real source of your troubles.

Friend, if you will lift your eyes of faith and begin to believe the truth — that God only gives good, beneficial, and profitable things that bring maturity to your life — you will begin to see how He is showering you with a continual downpour of good and perfect gifts.

God's Good Character Is Something That Never Changes

As James completed verse 17, he specifically said that the good and perfect gifts from above are "…from the Father of lights…." Again, he used comparative language. In this case, James compared what comes from the Father of *lights* (God) verses what comes from the father of *darkness* (Satan).

James continued on to describe the Father of lights as one "…with whom is no variableness neither shadow of turning." When we look at this wording in the original Greek text, we find language that was used to describe a Roman sundial. This was a stone that had a piece of metal affixed to the center and numbers carved into it that were arranged in a circular fashion. The sundial served as a clock to indicate the hours of the day.

As the earth moved and rotated, the shadow would shift and fall on the number indicating what time of day it was. Thus, the shadow was always shifting and changing. This imagery describing the Roman sundial is what James used to describe the character of God. Unlike the sundial, when it comes to what God gives and what He never gives, *God never changes* — He is absolutely fixed. On this question, you never have to wonder or speculate. If what you're experiencing is something horrible, you can be sure that it was *not* sent from God.

During those times of distress, the enemy wants you to think, *Well, maybe God has made an exception this time* — but that's a lie. Remove those kinds of thoughts from your mind because they will destroy you. Instead, get into God's Word and renew your mind with this truth in James 1:17: "Every good gift and every perfect gift is from above, and cometh down from the Father of lights, with whom is no variableness, neither shadow of turning."

In our next lesson, we are going to talk about how disobedience is another reason bad things happen in our lives.

STUDY QUESTIONS

> Study to shew thyself approved unto God, a workman that needeth not to be ashamed, rightly dividing the word of truth.
> — 2 Timothy 2:15

1. Knowing the truth is priceless! According to John 14:6, to know the truth is to know Jesus. Indeed, there are some extraordinary blessings that result from studying and learning the truth. What blessings can you identify in these words of Jesus?

   > **…Be careful what you are hearing. The measure [of thought and study] you give [to the truth you hear] will be the measure of virtue and knowledge] that comes back to you — and more [besides] will be given to you who hear.**
   > **— Mark 4:24 (*AMPC*)**

   > **…If you abide in My word [hold fast to My teachings and live in accordance with them], you are truly My disciples. And you will know the Truth, and the Truth will set you free.**
   > **— John 8:31,32 (*AMPC*)**

   > **The seed that fell on good soil represents those who truly hear and understand God's word and produce a harvest of thirty, sixty, or even a hundred times as much as had been planted!**
   > **— Matthew 13:23 (*NLT*)**

   Are you experiencing these kinds of results in your life? What can you do to make more time for the truth and see God's blessing increase in your life?

2. In the program, Rick gave an example of how a poverty mindset greatly affected him and the life of his family. What do you believe is God's will regarding your financial state as a believer? If you are unsure or lack knowledge in this area, consider the following passages from Scripture:

   - 3 John 2
   - Proverbs 10:22

- Luke 6:38; Malachi 3:10; John 10:10
- 2 Corinthians 9:8-11

What is the Holy Spirit showing you in these verses?

PRACTICAL APPLICATION

> But be ye doers of the word, and not hearers only, deceiving your own selves.
> —James 1:22

1. In what area(s) do you struggle with anxiety or worry because you lack knowledge of the truth? Is it *physical healing? Financial provision? The knowledge of God's love or how He sees you?* Let your wondering motivate you to get into God's Word so that you can learn and grow in the knowledge of the truth! As you spend time in His presence, look up scriptures pertaining to those subjects in your Bible concordance or an online search engine so you will receive knowledge of the truth to dispel the enemy's lies. Write down those scriptures and begin to meditate on them so they go deep into your heart.

2. Take some time to slow down and read again the sections in this lesson that explain the true meaning of James 1:13 and 17. What are your greatest takeaways from the meaning of these verses in the original Greek? How do these truths about what God always gives and what He never gives change your view of Him and the source of your problems?

LESSON 3

TOPIC

Disobedience Opens the Door to Bad Things

SCRIPTURES

1. **Isaiah 1:19** — If ye be willing and obedient, ye shall eat the good of the land.

2. **Deuteronomy 28:1-13** — And it shall come to pass, if thou shalt hearken diligently unto the voice of the Lord thy God, to observe and to do all his commandments which I command thee this day, that the Lord thy God will set thee on high above all nations of the earth: And all these blessings shall come on thee, and overtake thee, if thou shalt hearken unto the voice of the Lord thy God. Blessed shalt thou be in the city, and blessed shalt thou be in the field. Blessed shall be the fruit of thy body, and the fruit of thy ground, and the fruit of thy cattle, the increase of thy kine, and the flocks of thy sheep. Blessed shall be thy basket and thy store. Blessed shalt thou be when thou comest in, and blessed shalt thou be when thou goest out. The Lord shall cause thine enemies that rise up against thee to be smitten before thy face: they shall come out against thee one way, and flee before thee seven ways. The Lord shall command the blessing upon thee in thy storehouses, and in all that thou settest thine hand unto; and he shall bless thee in the land which the Lord thy God giveth thee. The Lord shall establish thee an holy people unto himself, as he hath sworn unto thee, if thou shalt keep the commandments of the Lord thy God, and walk in his ways. And all people of the earth shall see that thou art called by the name of the Lord; and they shall be afraid of thee. And the Lord shall make thee plenteous in goods, in the fruit of thy body, and in the fruit of thy cattle, and in the fruit of thy ground, in the land which the Lord sware unto thy fathers to give thee. The Lord shall open unto thee his good treasure, the heaven to give the rain unto thy land in his season, and to bless all the work of thine hand: and thou shalt lend unto many nations, and thou shalt not borrow. And the Lord shall make thee the head, and not the tail; and thou shalt be above only, and thou shalt not be beneath; if that thou hearken unto the commandments of the Lord thy God, which I command thee this day, to observe and to do them.

3. **Deuteronomy 28:15-35** — But it shall come to pass, if thou wilt not hearken unto the voice of the Lord thy God, to observe to do all his commandments and his statutes which I command thee this day; that all these curses shall come upon thee, and overtake thee: Cursed shalt thou be in the city, and cursed shalt thou be in the field. Cursed shall be thy basket and thy store. Cursed shall be the fruit of thy body, and the fruit of thy land, the increase of thy kine, and the flocks of thy sheep. Cursed shalt thou be when thou comest in, and cursed shalt thou be when thou goest out. The Lord shall send upon thee cursing,

vexation, and rebuke, in all that thou settest thine hand unto for to do, until thou be destroyed, and until thou perish quickly; because of the wickedness of thy doings, whereby thou hast forsaken me. The Lord shall make the pestilence cleave unto thee, until he have consumed thee from off the land, whither thou goest to possess it. The Lord shall smite thee with a consumption, and with a fever, and with an inflammation, and with an extreme burning, and with the sword, and with blasting, and with mildew; and they shall pursue thee until thou perish. And thy heaven that is over thy head shall be brass, and the earth that is under thee shall be iron. The Lord shall make the rain of thy land powder and dust: from heaven shall it come down upon thee, until thou be destroyed. The Lord shall cause thee to be smitten before thine enemies: thou shalt go out one way against them, and flee seven ways before them: and shalt be removed into all the kingdoms of the earth. And thy carcase shall be meat unto all fowls of the air, and unto the beasts of the earth, and no man shall fray them away. The Lord will smite thee with the botch of Egypt, and with the emerods, and with the scab, and with the itch, whereof thou canst not be healed. The Lord shall smite thee with madness, and blindness, and astonishment of heart: And thou shalt grope at noonday, as the blind gropeth in darkness, and thou shalt not prosper in thy ways: and thou shalt be only oppressed and spoiled evermore, and no man shall save thee. Thou shalt betroth a wife, and another man shall lie with her: thou shalt build an house, and thou shalt not dwell therein: thou shalt plant a vineyard, and shalt not gather the grapes thereof. Thine ox shall be slain before thine eyes, and thou shalt not eat thereof: thine ass shall be violently taken away from before thy face, and shall not be restored to thee: thy sheep shall be given unto thine enemies, and thou shalt have none to rescue them. Thy sons and thy daughters shall be given unto another people, and thine eyes shall look, and fail with longing for them all the day long; and there shall be no might in thine hand. The fruit of thy land, and all thy labours, shall a nation which thou knowest not eat up; and thou shalt be only oppressed and crushed alway: So that thou shalt be mad for the sight of thine eyes which thou shalt see. The Lord shall smite thee in the knees, and in the legs, with a sore botch that cannot be healed, from the sole of thy foot unto the top of thy head.

4. **Deuteronomy 28:38-45** — Thou shalt carry much seed out into the field, and shalt gather but little in; for the locust shall consume it.

Thou shalt plant vineyards, and dress them, but shalt neither drink of the wine, nor gather the grapes; for the worms shall eat them. Thou shalt have olive trees throughout all thy coasts, but thou shalt not anoint thyself with the oil; for thine olive shall cast his fruit. Thou shalt beget sons and daughters, but thou shalt not enjoy them; for they shall go into captivity. All thy trees and fruit of thy land shall the locust consume. The stranger that is within thee shall get up above thee very high; and thou shalt come down very low. He shall lend to thee, and thou shalt not lend to him: he shall be the head, and thou shalt be the tail. Moreover all these curses shall come upon thee, and shall pursue thee, and overtake thee, till thou be destroyed; because thou hearkenedst not unto the voice of the Lord thy God, to keep his commandments and his statutes which he commanded thee.

HEBREW WORDS

1. "if" — אִם (*im*): a hypothetical particle
2. "willing" — אָבָה (*abah*): willing to consent or to be willing
3. "obedient" — עָמַשׁ (*shama*): to hear and obey what has been spoken; the first part of obedience is hearing
4. "eat" — לָכַא (*akal*): to consume, devour, dine, eat, or feed
5. "good" — בוט (*tub*): best, best things, bounty, goods, goodness, good things, or prosperity

SYNOPSIS

So far, we have examined two reasons bad things happen to good people. The first and primary cause is due to the curse that was brought on the earth through Adam and Eve's sin. The moment they disobeyed God's Word, everything changed. The door was opened to the devil and death came rushing into the planet. As we saw previously in Romans 5:17, death began to reign like a king, and it did so up until Jesus' death on the Cross and His resurrection. Today, through faith in Him, we have the supernatural ability to override the curse and everything this fallen world throws at us.

The second reason bad things happen in people's lives is because they lack knowledge. What you believe to be true is vital and must line up with the Word of God for you to walk in victory. If you lack knowledge of the truth, you will believe the enemy's lies and open the door to problems in your life.

A third cause for calamities and problems is *disobedience*. When we disobey God's Word, we open the door for the enemy's activity in our life. On the other hand, when we obey God's Word, we will experience all the blessings He has promised us in His Word.

The emphasis of this lesson:

Disobedience opens the door for problems in our life. In contrast, when we hear and obey God's instructions, we position ourselves under His protection and experience His blessings. Deuteronomy 28 provides 14 verses on the blessings of obedience and 54 verses on the effects of disobedience.

Being 'Willing and Obedient' Opens the Door to God's Blessings

In Isaiah 1:19, God tells us, "If ye be willing and obedient, ye shall eat the good of the land." Indeed, this is a wonderful promise, but there is a condition that must be met. In order to experience its fulfillment, we must be *willing* and *obedient*.

The first word "if" is the Hebrew word *im*, which is a hypothetical particle, creating a hypothetical situation. To receive God's blessing, we must first be "willing." This is a translation of the Hebrew term *abah*, which means *willing to consent* or *to be willing*. The word "obedient" — the Hebrew word *shama* — means *to hear and obey what has been spoken*. Hence, the first part of obedience is hearing, and the second part is acting or doing what we are instructed to do.

If we are willing to consent to what God says and be obedient in hearing and doing it, God promises, "…Ye shall eat the good of the land" (Isaiah 1:19). The word "eat" in Hebrew is *akal*, which means *to consume, devour, dine, eat,* or *feed*. God says that you will feast on the good of the land if you are obedient.

This brings us to the word "good," which is the Hebrew word *tub*, and it describes what is *best* or *the best things*. It's the term for *bounty, goods, goodness, good things,* or *prosperity*. IF you are living a life of obedience, you should be experiencing good things and prosperity in your life. Of course, that doesn't mean you will have a problem-free life, because the devil is always trying to steal, kill, and destroy anything he can. Nevertheless, regularly experiencing God's goodness is a fruit of living in obedience to God.

Obedience Means Hearing and Doing What God Says

To really help us grasp the kind of blessings that come from living in obedience, God gives us an illustration of what we can expect in Deuteronomy 28. Although some will argue that this Old Testament passage relates to the Law of Moses, the principles it contains still apply to us. If we are willing and obedient, we will experience good things in our life as a result.

Deuteronomy 28:1 says, "And it shall come to pass, if thou shalt hearken diligently unto the voice of the Lord thy God, to observe and to do all his commandments which I command thee this day, that the Lord thy God will set thee on high above all nations of the earth."

Notice that within the first few words of this passage, we see the word "if" — the same hypothetical particle we saw in Isaiah 1:19. Again, this word creates a hypothetical situation. The verse then declares our part in the process in order to experience God's blessings — the first of which is that we "…hearken diligently unto the voice of the Lord thy God, to observe and to do all his commandments…."

Here again we see that *obedience* means that we *hear* God's instruction and *do* it. It is not enough to just hear from God; we must also take action and carry out what He tells us to do. When we both hear and do what God says, we will experience His promises. For Israel, the promise was: "…That the Lord thy God will set thee on high above all nations of the earth." For us, this indicates that when we are obedient, the result will be that God will promote us to a place of prominence.

God's Blessings for the Obedient in Deuteronomy 28:2-13

In Deuteronomy 28:2-13, Moses continued to speak on God's behalf to the people of Israel, laying out before them a list of blessings they could expect if they would be obedient to His commands. How do these promises apply to us? Let's read through the verses to find out.

Deuteronomy 28:2 tells us, "And all these blessings shall come on thee, and overtake thee, if thou shalt hearken unto the voice of the Lord thy God." Wow! How would you like to live a life in which God's blessings chase you down and overtake you? You can! That is God's promise to you when you are obedient.

Deuteronomy 28:3 says, "Blessed shalt thou be in the city, and blessed shalt thou be in the field." This seems to indicate that you will experience blessings in the marketplace where you shop (the city) and in the area of your work or employment (the field).

Deuteronomy 28:4 declares, "Blessed shall be the fruit of thy body, and the fruit of thy ground, and the fruit of thy cattle, the increase of thy kine, and the flocks of thy sheep." This means your body is going to be in good shape, you're going to have good health, and your unborn offspring will be healthy as well. The other references in this verse apply to everything you own being blessed, which includes your territory, and all your property. All of these areas will be blessed as a result of your obedience.

Deuteronomy 28:5,6 tells us, "Blessed shall be thy basket and thy store. Blessed shalt thou be when thou comest in, and blessed shalt thou be when thou goest out." The words "basket and store" refer to your income and your savings, and verse 6 says when you are obedient to God, you'll be blessed while coming and going!

Deuteronomy 28:7 states, "The Lord shall cause thine enemies that rise up against thee to be smitten before thy face: they shall come out against thee one way, and flee before thee seven ways." Notice, it doesn't say you won't have enemies. Instead, it says the Lord will cause your enemies to be *smitten before your face*, and the word "smitten" means *to slap*. Thus, when you are living in obedience, God promises to slap your enemies in the face and cause them to run from you seven ways.

Deuteronomy 28:8 says, "The Lord shall command the blessing upon thee in thy storehouses, and in all that thou settest thine hand unto; and he shall bless thee in the land which the Lord thy God giveth thee." Blessings on your "storehouses" is blessings on your savings account. And how would you like *everything* your hand touches to be blessed? That's another promise from God when you're obedient.

Deuteronomy 28:9 declares, "The Lord shall establish thee an holy people unto himself, as he hath sworn unto thee, if thou shalt keep the commandments of the Lord thy God, and walk in his ways." You will be firmly established by the Lord in everything that is good when you walk in obedience to His will.

Deuteronomy 28:10 states that "...All people of the earth shall see that thou art called by the name of the Lord; and they shall be afraid of thee." Here, God's promise to the obedient is that all people of the world will see how blessed we are and know that we belong to God, and it will cause them to view us with awe and wonder.

Deuteronomy 28:11 says, "And the Lord shall make thee plenteous in goods, in the fruit of thy body, and in the fruit of thy cattle, and in the fruit of thy ground, in the land which the Lord sware unto thy fathers to give thee." The phrase "plenteous in goods" means the obedient will be blessed with material possessions, and as we saw in verse 4, the blessings of "the fruit of thy body, the fruit of thy cattle, and the fruit of thy ground" reiterate God's blessings of multiplication in every area of your life.

Deuteronomy 28:12 tells us, "The Lord shall open unto thee his good treasure, the heaven to give the rain unto thy land in his season, and to bless all the work of thine hand: and thou shalt lend unto many nations, and thou shalt not borrow." Obedient living will cause God to make His personal treasures in Heaven available to you and send forth prosperity so you can be a blessing to others!

Deuteronomy 28:13 declares, "And the Lord shall make thee the head, and not the tail; and thou shalt be above only, and thou shalt not be beneath; if that thou hearken unto the commandments of the Lord thy God, which I command thee this day, to observe and to do them." Here, God reveals that obedience will cause you to stand out as a leader among men.

All of these verses speak of God's blessings to the obedient. When we come to Deuteronomy 28:14, Moses reminds the people once more of their part in the agreement: "And thou shalt not go aside from any of the words which I command thee this day, to the right hand, or to the left, to go after other gods to serve them."

The Effects of Disobedience in Deuteronomy 28:15-45

Now when most people read Deuteronomy 28, they stop at verse 14. But to get the full message of what God is communicating, we need to continue reading to the end of the chapter. The fact is, there are 14 verses on the blessings of obedience, and there are 54 verses that talk about the effects of disobedience.

As Moses continued speaking on behalf of God, he said, "But it shall come to pass, if thou wilt *not* hearken unto the voice of the Lord thy God, to observe to do all his commandments and his statutes which I command thee this day; that all these curses shall come upon thee, and overtake thee" (Deuteronomy 28:15).

To be clear, this verse doesn't say that God is going to curse you. Remember, there is a curse already at work in the world because of Adam's disobedience. If you walk in obedience, you can live your life above that curse. Through Jesus, you have been given a faith that has the power to subdue every force in the world that is working against you, including the curse. However, if you walk in disobedience, you subject yourself to that curse instead of putting *it* in subjection to *you*. That is why Moses reminded the people that if they weren't obedient, curses would come upon them and overtake them.

The following are some of the curses mentioned in **Deuteronomy 28** of what God cautioned the Israelites would happen if they were not obedient to His commands:

> Verse 16: Cursed shalt thou be in the city, and cursed shalt thou be in the field.
>
> Verse 17: Cursed shall be thy basket and thy store.
>
> Verse 18: Cursed shall be the fruit of thy body, and the fruit of thy land, the increase of thy kine, and the flocks of thy sheep.
>
> Verse 19: Cursed shalt thou be when thou comest in, and cursed shalt thou be when thou goest out.
>
> Verse 20: The Lord shall send upon thee cursing, vexation, and rebuke, in all that thou settest thine hand unto for to do, until thou be destroyed, and until thou perish quickly; because of the wickedness of thy doings, whereby thou hast forsaken me.
>
> Verse 21: The Lord shall make the pestilence cleave unto thee, until he have consumed thee from off the land, whither thou goest to possess it.

Friend, all of these horrible things are in the world because of the curse. When you are walking in obedience to the Lord and His Word, you are able to ride above it all. But when you walk in disobedience, you are opening the door for these things to come flooding into your life, just as it did when Adam and Eve disobeyed the Lord.

Continuing on in Deuteronomy 28:

> Verse 22: The Lord shall smite thee with a consumption, and with a fever, and with an inflammation, and with an extreme burning, and with the sword, and with blasting, and with mildew; and they shall pursue thee until thou perish.
>
> Verse 23: And thy heaven that is over thy head shall be brass, and the earth that is under thee shall be iron.
>
> Verse 24: The Lord shall make the rain of thy land powder and dust: from heaven shall it come down upon thee, until thou be destroyed.
>
> Verse 25: The Lord shall cause thee to be smitten before thine enemies: thou shalt go out one way against them, and flee seven ways before them: and shalt be removed into all the kingdoms of the earth.

These things are not the will of God for your life and that is why He doesn't want you to walk in disobedience. So considering these things — is it better to walk in obedience or disobedience?

> Verse 26: And thy carcase shall be meat unto all fowls of the air, and unto the beasts of the earth, and no man shall fray them away.
>
> Verse 27: The Lord will smite thee with the botch of Egypt, and with the emerods, and with the scab, and with the itch, whereof thou canst not be healed.
>
> Verse 28: The Lord shall smite thee with madness, and blindness, and astonishment of heart:
>
> Verse 29: And thou shalt grope at noonday, as the blind gropeth in darkness, and thou shalt not prosper in thy ways: and thou shalt be only oppressed and spoiled evermore, and no man shall save thee.
>
> Verse 30: Thou shalt betroth a wife, and another man shall lie with her: thou shalt build an house, and thou shalt not dwell

therein: thou shalt plant a vineyard, and shalt not gather the grapes thereof.

Verse 31: Thine ox shall be slain before thine eyes, and thou shalt not eat thereof: thine ass shall be violently taken away from before thy face, and shall not be restored to thee: thy sheep shall be given unto thine enemies, and thou shalt have none to rescue them.

Verse 32: Thy sons and thy daughters shall be given unto another people, and thine eyes shall look, and fail with longing for them all the day long; and there shall be no might in thine hand.

Verse 33: The fruit of thy land, and all thy labours, shall a nation which thou knowest not eat up; and thou shalt be only oppressed and crushed alway:

Verse 34: So that thou shalt be mad for the sight of thine eyes which thou shalt see.

Verse 35: The Lord shall smite thee in the knees, and in the legs, with a sore botch that cannot be healed, from the sole of thy foot unto the top of thy head.

Verse 36: The Lord shall bring thee, and thy king which thou shalt set over thee, unto a nation which neither thou nor thy fathers have known; and there shalt thou serve other gods, wood and stone.

Verse 37: And thou shalt become an astonishment, a proverb, and a byword, among all nations whither the Lord shall lead thee.

Verse 38: Thou shalt carry much seed out into the field, and shalt gather but little in; for the locust shall consume it.

Verse 39: Thou shalt plant vineyards, and dress them, but shalt neither drink of the wine, nor gather the grapes; for the worms shall eat them.

Verse 40: Thou shalt have olive trees throughout all thy coasts, but thou shalt not anoint thyself with the oil; for thine olive shall cast his fruit.

Verse 41: Thou shalt beget sons and daughters, but thou shalt not enjoy them; for they shall go into captivity.

Verse 42: All thy trees and fruit of thy land shall the locust consume.

Verse 43: The stranger that is within thee shall get up above thee very high; and thou shalt come down very low.

Verse 44: He shall lend to thee, and thou shalt not lend to him: he shall be the head, and thou shalt be the tail.

Verse 45: Moreover all these curses shall come upon thee, and shall pursue thee, and overtake thee, till thou be destroyed; because thou hearkenedst not unto the voice of the Lord thy God, to keep his commandments and his statutes which he commanded thee.

There are 28 more verses in this chapter that reveal the negative effects that result from disobedience. All of these horrible things are at work in the world because of the curse caused by Adam and Eve's sin. When you walk in obedience, you submit yourself to the authority of God and receive the power of God to rise above it all. But if you walk in disobedience, you open the door for these things to come rushing into your life — none of which are God's will for you.

The Choice Is Yours: Blessings or Curses

Just like with the people of Israel, God's instruction is clear: When we are willing and obedient, we will walk in His blessing and prosperity. But when we are disobedient to His Word, we come out from under His protection and experience all kinds of disastrous things in our life — the kinds of things described in Deuteronomy 28:15-68 that result from the curse.

If you are experiencing any of these hurtful, damaging things in your life, don't automatically assume it's the devil. First, pause and pray, asking the Lord to search your heart and mind to see if there are any areas in which you are walking in disobedience. If He shows you disobedience in your life, repent so that you slam the door on the devil and the curse. You will know in your heart if you are walking in disobedience, so be quick to acknowledge it and repent.

Repentance allows us to get back under God's protection and causes all of those curses and negative things to stop, and when we get back on the right side of obedience, we will see God's blessings begin to flow in our life again. Remember, in Isaiah 1:19, God declares, "If ye be willing and obedient, ye shall eat the good of the land."

Again, the first word "if" in Hebrew is a hypothetical particle, creating a hypothetical situation. To receive God's blessing, we must first be "willing." This is the Hebrew term *abah*, meaning *willing to consent* or *to be willing*. And the word "obedient" means *to hear and obey what has been spoken*. Hence, the first part of obedience is hearing, and the second part is doing what we've been instructed to do.

If you are willing to consent to what God says and to be obedient in hearing and doing His Word, He promises, "…Ye shall eat the good of the land" (Isaiah 1:19). The word "eat" means *to consume, devour, dine, eat*, or *feed*. God says that you will feast on the good of the land as a result of your obedience.

Friend, this is a principle that applies to the whole Word of God. When you obey, all kinds of good things will come on you and overtake you, but when you disobey, you will receive bad things instead. Again, the word "good" describes what is *best* or *the best things*. It is the term for *bounty, goods, goodness, good things*, or *prosperity*. IF you live a life of obedience, you will experience the blessings of God. But if you disobey and refuse to do what He has said, the door to your life will be opened for all kinds of bad things to come rushing in.

As Moses said to the children of Israel more than 3,000 years ago, God is also saying to us today: "I call heaven and earth to record this day against you, that I have set before you life and death, blessing and cursing: therefore choose life, that both thou and thy seed may live" (Deuteronomy 30:19). In the end, *it always pays to obey*.

STUDY QUESTIONS

Study to shew thyself approved unto God, a workman that needeth not to be ashamed, rightly dividing the word of truth.
— 2 Timothy 2:15

1. Take time to carefully read through Deuteronomy 28:1-13, which speaks of the many blessings we can experience when we obey God's Word. Out of all these blessings, which ones excite you and speak to your heart the most? Which of these are you personally experiencing?
2. What else does God say in His Word about obedience? Meditate on these scriptures and write in what is missing in the blanks.
   - **Proverbs 3:1,2** – Obeying the Word adds _____, _____, and _____.
   - **1 Samuel 15:22** – Obedience is better than _____ in God's eyes.
   - **Acts 5:29** – There comes a time when we must obey God rather than _____.
   - **1 Kings 3:14** – When we walk in obedience, God promises _____.
   - **2 Corinthians 10:5** – We must take our _____ captive in obedience to the _____.
   - **James 1:22** – If we do not obey the Word, we are _____ ourselves.

PRACTICAL APPLICATION

> But be ye doers of the word, and not hearers only, deceiving your own selves.
> —James 1:22

1. Disobedience opens the door to the curse that is already at work in the earth as a result of Adam and Eve's sin. As you take time to continue reading Deuteronomy 28:15-68, what consequences of disobedience are the most concerning and disturbing to you? Why?
2. Are you experiencing any of these hurtful, damaging things in your life? If you are, which ones? Get alone in the Lord's presence and pray, "Lord, search my heart and mind and show me if there are any areas where I am walking in disobedience" (*see* Psalm 139:23,24). Now be still and listen. What is He revealing? If He shows you something, repent (*see* 1 John 1:9). In doing so, you will slam the door on the devil and the curse.

LESSON 4

TOPIC
Stupidity Opens the Door to Bad Things

SCRIPTURES

1. **Galatians 6:7** — Be not deceived; God is not mocked: for whatsoever a man soweth, that shall he also reap. For he that soweth to his flesh shall of the flesh reap corruption; but he that soweth to the Spirit shall of the Spirit reap life everlasting.
2. **Hosea 4:6** — My people are destroyed for lack of knowledge....

HEBREW WORDS

1. "destroyed" — הָמָה (*damah*): to cease, to cause to cease, to cut off, to destroy, to perish, to be silenced, to be undone, to be brought to destruction, or to be brought to ruin
2. "knowledge" — תַּעַד (*daath*): knowledge; perception; truth; pictures one who is ignorant, unaware, or unknowledgeable

GREEK WORDS

1. "deceived" — πλανάω (*planao*): to lead astray
2. "mocked" — μυκτηρίζω (*mukteridzo*): to turn one's nose up at someone; to disdain; to show contempt; to scorn; to sneer at someone; to mock
3. "whatsoever" — ὅ (*ho*): whatever; referring to anything at all
4. "soweth" — σπείρω (*speiro*): to scatter or to sow, as in sowing seed
5. "that" — τοῦτο (*touto*): this, this exactly, meaning the same thing he sowed
6. "reap" — θερίζω (*theridzo*): to harvest or reap
7. "soweth" — σπείρω (*speiro*): to scatter or to sow, as in sowing seed; here it means continuously sowing
8. "to" — εἰς (*eis*): into

9. "the flesh" — τὴν σάρκα ἑαυτοῦ (*ten sarka heautou*): his own flesh; the flesh of himself
10. "of" — ἐκ (*ek*): out; out of; directly out of
11. "flesh" — σαρκὸς (*sarkos*): the flesh; the flesh realm
12. "reap" — θερίζω (*theridzo*): to harvest or reap
13. "corruption" — φθορά (*phthora*): corruption, decay, or rottenness; depicts that which is putrid
14. "but" — δὲ (*de*): a particle intended to make a transition to a dramatic point
15. "soweth" — σπείρω (*speiro*): to scatter or to sow, as in sowing seed; here it means continuously sowing
16. "the Spirit" — τὸ Πνεῦμα (*to Pneuma*): to the Spirit or into the Spirit
17. "of" — ἐκ (*ek*): out; out of; directly out of
18. "reap" — θερίζω (*theridzo*): to harvest or reap
19. "life everlasting" — ζωὴν αἰώνιον (*zoen aionion*): life everlasting; life that is immeasurable

SYNOPSIS

So far, we have looked at three primary reasons bad things happen to good people or why bad things happen for any reason. In our first lesson, we identified the main culprit that causes problems in our lives, and that is *the curse* that came upon everyone and everything in the world because of Adam and Eve's sin.

When Adam and Eve disobeyed God, a spiritual door was opened to the devil and death came raging into the world. According to Romans 5, death began to reign like a king over everything connected to the earth realm. Thankfully, God mercifully intervened and sent His Son, Jesus, whose death on the Cross and resurrection stripped death of its power. Now through faith in Him, we have the divine ability to exercise our faith and rise above the effects of the curse!

Then we saw that the second major reason for problems is *a lack of knowledge*. If we don't have the knowledge of God's Word, we become cut off from things like His healing, wisdom, peace, prosperity, and so many other blessings. We need to know and operate in the knowledge of the truth to avoid coming to ruin in our life.

And in our third lesson, we found out that another cause for bad things happening is *disobedience*. Disobedience keeps us from living the best life God intended for us to have, and it opens us up to all kinds of tragedy and trauma. In contrast, obedience enables us to rise above it all and experience the blessings of God. His Word promises, "If you are willing and obedient, you shall eat the good of the land" (Isaiah 1:19 *NKJV*).

The emphasis of this lesson:

Many times, the problems we face are a result of our own foolishness, or in layman's terms, our own stupidity. Whether it's our health, our finances, our relationships, or another area of our life, everything we do is like a seed we are sowing that will produce a harvest. Continually making bad decisions will yield bad things for us, but consistently making good decisions will bring good things into our life.

Stupidity Opens the Door to Difficulties and Struggles

The fourth major reason bad things happen to people is simply *stupidity*. Although we may not want to admit it, our own stupidity is often what opens the door to experiencing problems. Consider these examples that are more common than you may think:

Some people have financial difficulties because they do stupid things with their money. They keep using their credit cards, buying things they don't need and can't pay for, all the while being oblivious to the money they're wasting. Then they say things like, "The devil's messing with my finances," or "I guess it's just not God's will for me to be blessed with prosperity like others." But the truth is, they've made some stupid decisions regarding their finances, and that's why they're in a financial mess.

Some people can't keep a job because they don't respect authority or they have a bad work ethic. If a person is unwilling to get along with their boss and coworkers and they do mediocre work at best, they're going to lose job after job. Eventually, their resume of past employment will tarnish their reputation to the point that no one will want to hire them. Their own foolish choices will have caused hardship in their potential for work.

Some people get sick because they don't take care of themselves. Right now, there are individuals who are dealing with chronic health challenges like diabetes, joint pain, or other physical issues, and a major cause for those things is unhealthy eating habits and a lack of exercise. They likely eat too many sugary foods and drinks and fail to drink enough water and get the proper amounts of protein and nutrients in their meals.

Strangely, these people say things like, "Well, I guess it's God's will for me to struggle in my health. It is just my lot in life." But the truth is they have done very little to take care of their body, and that is why they're sick. Their condition has nothing to do with God. It is because of their own unwise decisions.

Some people have become immobilized because of repeatedly making poor choices. Rather than make an effort to get up and regularly move and be active, they choose to just sit on the couch or in a chair all day, watching TV, scrolling on their phone, and eating whatever they want. Then they say things like, "Well, I guess it's God's will that I'm sick and stuck at home."

Friend, a person can't live like that and expect to be healthy. If you don't move physically, you will lose the ability to move. Although it is *not* God's will that you or anyone else be sick and disabled, if you eat poorly, don't exercise, don't get good rest, and fail to take care of yourself, you're going to experience all kinds of physical problems. You can request prayer, go to the doctor, and throw medication at your symptoms, but if you don't take care of your physical body, you're not going to have the kind of health God wants you to have.

Rick shared in the program that he also had to come to grips with some foolish choices he was making. He said how years ago he went through a time when he was overweight and struggled with his eating. But the Lord showed him that he couldn't keep eating the way he was eating, not exercising — living a sedentary lifestyle — and expect to be healthy. The same is true for you. If you keep eating poorly and remain inactive, your physical body is going to continue to get bigger and bigger. It's just a fact.

It's not the devil's fault, the world's fault, or God's fault. It's your own fault, and the responsibility stops at your doorstep. Although not every health problem can be avoided, many of the challenges people are facing can be prevented by simply making wiser decisions. If you've made some stupid choices, repent and ask God to forgive you, and begin making wise choices that lead to the life God intended for you to have.

God Is Not 'Mocked': What You Sow, You Will Reap

If we stop and think about it, all our actions are subject to *the law of sowing and reaping*. Even unsaved people in the world are aware of this principle and know that it cannot be circumvented. "What goes around comes around," as they say. Like the law of gravity, the law of sowing and reaping always works and cannot be denied.

Here is the way the Holy Spirit communicated this universal principle through the apostle Paul:

> **Be not deceived; God is not mocked: for whatsoever a man soweth, that shall he also reap.**
> — Galatians 6:7

Although many people quote this verse in the context of giving, which it certainly does relate to, this law applies to *everything* we do.

First, notice the word "deceived." It is the Greek word *planao*, and it basically means *to lead astray*. When Paul said, "Be not deceived," a better translation would be, "Don't let anyone lead you astray with what you're about to hear." Then he continued in that verse by saying, "…God is not mocked…."

In Greek, the word "mocked" is *mukteridzo*, and it means *to turn one's nose up at someone*. It can also mean *to disdain, to show contempt, to scorn, to sneer at someone*, or *to mock*. In the context of this verse, it carries the idea of someone saying to God, "Well, this may apply to everyone else, but it doesn't apply to me." It is this arrogant attitude that prompted Paul to strongly warn, "Don't be deceived — don't let anyone lead you astray on the issue I'm about to tell you."

He then added, "…For whatsoever a man soweth, that shall he also reap." The word "whatsoever" is the Greek word *ho*, and it means *whatever*, referring to *anything at all*. "Soweth" is a translation of the Greek word *speiro*, which means *to scatter or to sow, as in sowing seed*. Whatsoever we sow or plant as seed we are going to *reap* a harvest from.

In Greek, the word "reap" is *theridzo*, which means *to harvest or reap*. Thus, the law of sowing and reaping says anything and everything that you plant — whether good or bad — that is what you're going to reap. Interestingly, even the word "that" — the Greek word *touto* — is important, as it means *this* or *this exactly*. In other words, *the very same thing* you sow is what you are going to reap.

A Practical Application of the Law of Sowing and Reaping

Again, this divine principle applies to *every sphere* of life. If you plant financial seeds into your local church or a ministry that is spreading the Gospel and taking care of the poor, God promises that you will reap a harvest of finances and spiritual blessings. Likewise, if you plant *time*, *attention*, and *care* into people's lives, you will reap a harvest of the same in your relationships.

How you treat others will determine how you are treated.

Every *action* and *attitude* is a seed you are sowing from which you are going to harvest. If you sow kindness and mercy, you will reap kindness and mercy. If you sow time and attention, you will reap time and attention from others.

The opposite is also true. If you sow strife, bitterness, and unforgiveness toward others, strife, bitterness, and unforgiveness are what you will reap. Let's say someone has mistreated you in some way. In that case, you need to be careful to give them forgiveness and release them into God's hands, because one day soon you too may need forgiveness.

You must plant now what you know you are going to want to reap in the future.

Whatever you do to others is exactly what's going to be done to you. Likewise, whatever you do *not* do to others is exactly what's *not* going to be done to you. This is a very sobering principle we need to be aware of because it is guiding our life every day whether we realize it or not.

Again, Paul said, "Be not deceived; God is not mocked: for whatsoever a man soweth, that shall he also reap" (Galatians 6:7). In other words, "Don't be misled on the subject of sowing and reaping. God will not be mocked, so don't turn your nose up or scoff at Him as if this principle is not going to work in your life. Whatsoever you sow — *absolutely anything at all* — that is the exact same thing you are going to reap."

Now in a real practical sense, this means if you eat too much, you're going to gain too much weight. Similarly, if you eat the wrong things, you are going to reap a harvest of wrong results in your body. Everything has a specific cause and effect, because everything you do in life is a seed.

If you sit on the couch or a chair and never move, that is a seed you are sowing, and you're going to reap a harvest of immobility. If you sow the seed of not taking care of your physical health, then you're going to reap health problems. Likewise, if you don't sow time and attention into your marriage, you're going to reap marriage problems.

Is this starting to register in your mind and heart? Sowing and reaping is a universal law of God that applies to everyone — the saved and the unsaved. It doesn't matter where you grew up, how educated you are, or how much money you have. This law of God always works, and again, it is never denied.

When You Sow to the Flesh, You Will Reap 'Corruption'

Immediately after the apostle Paul wrote about the law of sowing and reaping, he added further explanation:

> **For he that soweth to his flesh shall of the flesh reap corruption; but he that soweth to the Spirit shall of the Spirit reap life everlasting.**
> **— Galatians 6:8**

Here again, we see the word "soweth" — the Greek word *speiro*, which means *to scatter or to sow, as in sowing seed*. In this verse, the verb tense indicates *continuously sowing*, which means we could translate the opening part of the verse, "For he that soweth and soweth and soweth and soweth to his flesh...."

In Greek, the words "his flesh" are a translation of the words *ten sarka heautou*, which literally means *his own flesh* or *the flesh of himself*. And the word "to" is the little Greek word *ois*, which means *into*. Hence, when a person sows and sows into his flesh, "...of the flesh [realm he will] reap corruption..." (Galatians 6:8).

The word "of" in Greek is *ek*, which means *out, out of,* or *directly out of*. If you are continuously sowing into your carnal nature, you are going to "reap corruption" directly out of the *realm* of the flesh because the second reference to "flesh" in that verse is the Greek word *sarkos* which refers to *the flesh realm*. We see the word "reap" for a second time in this passage — the Greek word *theridzo*, which means *to harvest or reap*, and the word "corruption" is the Greek word *phthora*. It describes *corruption*, *decay*, or *rottenness*. Moreover, it depicts *that which is putrid*, which means if you plant seeds into your flesh, you're going to reap *really stinking* situations in your life.

When You Sow to the Spirit, You Will Reap 'Life Everlasting'

In Galatians 6:8, Paul went on to say, "…But he that soweth to the Spirit shall of the Spirit reap life everlasting." The opening word "but" is the little Greek word *de*, and it is a particle intended to make a transition to a dramatic point. The point Paul is driving home here is that if you sow into the Spirit, you will reap a harvest of "life everlasting."

For a third time, we see the word "soweth" — the Greek word *speiro*, which means *to scatter* or *to sow, as in sowing seed*. Here it indicates *continuously sowing*. Thus, we could translate this part of the verse, "He that *soweth and soweth and soweth* to the Spirit shall of the Spirit reap life everlasting."

The phrase "the Spirit" is a translation of the Greek words *to Pneuma*, which means *to the Spirit* or *into the Spirit*. The word "of" is the little Greek word *ek*, which means *out*, *out of*, or *directly out of*, and again the word "reap" — the Greek word *theridzo* — means *to harvest or reap*. The use of all these terms tells us that when we continuously sow into the realm of the Spirit, directly out of the realm of the Spirit we will reap a harvest of "life everlasting."

The words "life everlasting" are a translation of the Greek words *zoen aionion*, which describe *life everlasting* or *life that is immeasurable*. So when you continue to sow positive, right actions into the realm of the Spirit, you are going to reap or receive an immeasurable, full, abundant life of positive things.

The Decision Is Yours: What Kind of Harvest Do You Want To Reap?

Now that we have explained the law of sowing and reaping, it is up to you to decide what kind of seed you're going to plant because that will determine what kind of harvest you're going to reap. Are you going to be wise or are you going to be foolish? If you make unwise, carnally-driven choices, you're sowing seed that will produce bad and potentially damaging results.

Friend, if you're dealing with difficult circumstances or situations right now, you need to pause and pray and be very honest with the Lord and with yourself. It may be that you're living in the harvest of bad seed that you planted in the past. If that is the case and you want to get rid of that harvest, you need to repent and pray that those bad seeds will not produce any fruit.

Through the act of repentance you close the door to an unwanted harvest. The Spirit of God will uproot those bad seeds, and you can begin planting positive, godly seeds that will produce great, healthy results in your life — a harvest of abundant life that is full of immeasurable good things.

Remember, in Hosea 4:6, God says, "My people are destroyed for lack of knowledge…." That word "destroyed" means *to cease, to cause to cease, to be cut off, to be destroyed, to perish, to be silenced, to be undone, to be brought to destruction*, or *to be brought to ruin*. Thus, people are destroyed, they perish, they're silenced, they're undone, they're brought to destruction, and they're ruined because of a lack of knowledge — they are unaware of the truth of God's Word.

In this lesson, you've received some very important insight from Galatians 6:7: "Be not deceived; God is not mocked: for whatsoever a man soweth, that shall he also reap." Anything and everything you plant is a seed that is going to produce a harvest. If you plant wrong actions and attitudes, you're going to receive a disastrous harvest. But if you continue to plant wise and honorable seeds, you will reap a harvest of good things.

On this principle, again, God is not mocked, so don't deceive yourself into thinking that somehow your life is an exception. This is a universal law that applies to each one of us. Therefore, *make sure you're planting the right seeds so you can reap a good harvest in your life!*

In our final lesson, we will explore how attacks from the devil open the door to bad things.

STUDY QUESTIONS

> Study to shew thyself approved unto God, a workman that needeth not to be ashamed, rightly dividing the word of truth.
> — 2 Timothy 2:15

1. Most believers agree that taking care of our spirit is important, but what about our physical body? What does the Bible say about taking care of it? Read through these scriptures and identify some of the key reasons we need to do our best to maintain the health and purity of our body.

    - 1 Corinthians 6:12,13,18-20
    - 2 Corinthians 6:16
    - Romans 12:1
    - Romans 6:12; 8:13
    - 1 Corinthians 10:31

2. Dedicating and consecrating our bodies to God is a biblical command. Romans 12:1 says, "I beseech you therefore, brethren, by the mercies of God, that ye present your *bodies* a living sacrifice, holy, acceptable unto God, which is your reasonable service." To help you better grasp what the Lord is saying, take time to reflect on Romans 12:1 and 2 in *The Message* version:

    So here's what I want you to do, God helping you: Take your everyday, ordinary life — your sleeping, eating, going-to-work, and walking-around life — and place it before God as an offering. Embracing what God does for you is the best thing you can do for him. Don't become so well-adjusted to your culture that you fit into it without even thinking. Instead, fix your attention on God. You'll be changed from the inside out. Readily recognize what he wants from you, and quickly respond to it. Unlike the culture around you, always dragging you down to its level of immaturity, God brings the best out of you, develops well-formed maturity in you.

What is the Holy Spirit speaking to your heart in this passage? Are there any adjustments you feel He is prompting you to make? If so, what are they?

PRACTICAL APPLICATION

> But be ye doers of the word, and not hearers only, deceiving your own selves.
> —James 1:22

1. After reading the explanation of the original Greek meaning of the law of sowing and reaping found in Galatians 6:7 and 8, what are your greatest conclusions? How does this understanding instill a healthy, reverential fear of the Lord in you and challenge you to come up higher in the way you live your life?
2. Always remember that every action and attitude is a seed you are sowing. It has a specific cause and effect from which you will reap a harvest. Be honest: is there something you're doing in your relationships, with your finances, on your job, with your health, or elsewhere that you know is "bad seed"? If so, what do you need to *stop* sowing and what do you need to *start* sowing to reap the blessings of God?
3. If you've made some stupid choices, take time now to repent and make things right with God. Pray, "*Lord, please forgive me for any wrong attitudes in my heart and actions that have opened the door for the curse to come on me instead of what Jesus died for me to have. I repent from* [name anything specific He shows you] *and I am asking you to uproot any bad seed I have planted so that I don't reap a harvest from it. Help me, Father. Give me Your grace to make smart, godly choices in every area of my life through the power of the Holy Spirit within me. I choose to present my body to You today and everyday as a living sacrifice. It is Your temple, and I want to honor You with it. Thank You for loving me and helping me to always be mindful of the law of sowing and reaping in every area of my life. In Jesus' name. Amen!*"

LESSON 5

TOPIC
Devilish Attacks Open the Door to Bad Things

SCRIPTURES
1. **1 Thessalonians 2:17,18** — But we, brethren, being taken from you for a short time in presence, not in heart, endeavoured the more abundantly to see your face with great desire. Wherefore we would have come unto you, even I Paul, once and again; but Satan hindered us.
2. **James 4:7** — Submit yourselves therefore to God. Resist the devil, and he will flee from you.

GREEK WORDS
1. "Satan" — Σατανᾶς (*satanas*): one who hates, accuses, slanders, or conspires against
2. "hindered" — ἐγκόπτω (*egkopto*): to cut in on; to elbow out of the way; to block a road; to create an impasse; to cause a disruption
3. "submit" — ὑποτάσσω (*hupotasso*): a compound of ὑπό (*hupo*) and τάσσω (*tasso*); the preposition ὑπό (*hupo*) means under, and the word τάσσω (*tasso*) means to arrange; as a compound, it means to properly arrange under, and it is a military term depicting a soldier's obedience and submission to authority; it signifies one who properly arranges himself under the authority of God and His Word; importantly, it pictures one who is submitted to authority as being under the covering and protection of a greater authority and who actually hides behind the authority of the one to whom he is submitted, and this tells us that there is protection in submission
4. "resist" — ἀνθίστημι (*anthistemi*): a compound of ἀντί (*anti*) and ἵστημι (*histemi*); the word ἀντί (*anti*) means against, and the word ἵστημι (*histemi*) means to stand; as a compound, it means to stand against or to stand in opposition; demonstrates the attitude of one who is fiercely opposed to something and therefore determines to do everything in his power to resist it; to defy, to stand against, or to

withstand; it depicts a well-thought-out and well-planned resistance; used in ancient Greece to picture the fierce resistance of an enemy

5. "devil" — διάβολος (*diabolos*): portrays one who is known to slander, accuse, or assault or one who tries to ensnare others in some kind of a net or trap

6. "flee" — φεύγω (*pheugo*): to flee, to take flight, to run away, to run as fast as possible, or to escape; pictures one's feet flying as he runs from a situation; used to depict a lawbreaker who flees in terror from a city or a nation where he broke the law; James states in this verse that when you submit to God and align yourself under His authority, you are empowered to successfully resist the devil and anything he brings against you, and in that consecrated position of submission, the devil will "flee" from you like a criminal who flees in terror after breaking the law

SYNOPSIS

When it comes to the reasons bad things happen in our lives, devilish attacks are certainly one of them. The Bible says, "For we wrestle not against flesh and blood, but against principalities, against powers, against the rulers of the darkness of this world, against spiritual wickedness in high places" (Ephesians 6:12). Indeed, our enemy Satan is real and he does come against us.

Thankfully, we have the power to defeat him because God has given us powerful spiritual weapons, including His all-powerful Word. To fight successfully in spiritual warfare, you must be spiritually strong. The Bible must be a central part of your daily life, and you must live in a position of submission to the authority of God so that you can overcome those attacks from the devil.

The emphasis of this lesson:

Sometimes the bad things that happen to us are the result of the devil's attacks. He and his minions work to create roadblocks, hindrances, and conspiracies to keep us from doing God's will. But as long as we stay in submission to God's authority, we have all the authority and power we need to effectively resist the devil and see him flee.

The Curse Is the Main Culprit for Bad Things Happening

Let's review what we have learned so far about why bad things happen to good people. In our first lesson, we learned that the *primary* reason bad things happen is because of the curse brought into the world through Adam and Eve's sin. Romans 5:12 says, "…By one man sin entered into the world, and death by sin; and so death passed upon all men…." When Adam disobeyed God, a spiritual door was opened, and evil came flooding into the planet.

When that occurred, Romans 5:17 tells us that death began reigning with kingly authority over everything, and the new law of darkness began to produce everything that was contrary to the life God had planned for man in the Garden. Genesis 3:18 says "thorns and thistles" emerged, which depicts *hurtful, dangerous situations* that are spinning out of control. Strife, wars, pestilence, sickness, earthquakes, tornadoes, hurricanes, and horrific climate issues are all the result of the curse coming upon the earth. Romans 8:22 gives us some insight into these events because it says, "…The whole creation groaneth and travaileth in pain together until now." The earth is waiting for the return of Christ who will ultimately liberate everything from the curse. But in the meantime, people are putting the blame on God for such things.

Although insurance companies often call natural disasters "acts of God," these tragic events have nothing to do with Him. In fact, blaming God for such terrible calamities is a form of taking the Lord's name in vain (*see* Exodus 20:7). The words "in vain" mean *ascribing blame to God for things He didn't do*. Ultimately, all the problems in the world could be laid at the feet of Adam because it was his disobedience that opened the door to death and the curse that came into the world.

Praise God, through the cross of Christ and what He accomplished by His death, burial, and resurrection, those of us who have received Him have been given authority over the enemy and a faith that overcomes the world (*see* 1 John 5:4). If we will learn how to walk in faith and operate in God's principles, we can override most of the effects of the curse.

Lack of Knowledge and Disobedience Also Open the Door for Problems

In our second lesson, we examined Hosea 4:6 where God says, "My people are destroyed for *lack of knowledge*...." When we insert the original Hebrew meaning of the word "destroyed" into this verse, we could translate it:

- My people are *caused to cease* and *are cut off* for a lack of knowledge....
- My people *are destroyed, they perish, they're silenced*, and *they're undone* for a lack of knowledge....
- My people *are brought to destruction* and *brought to ruin* for a lack of knowledge....

The second reason bad things happen in people's lives is *a lack of knowledge*. Make no mistake: when you lack knowledge of the truth of God's Word, it opens the door for destruction to enter your life. Therefore, you need to know what the Bible teaches — especially concerning what God always gives and what He never gives so you do not receive wrong things as though they are from Him. This knowledge will not only protect you but also empower you to experience the abundant life Jesus died to bring you (*see* John 10:10).

A third reason for bad things happening in people's lives is *disobedience*. If you walk in disobedience to the principles of God's Word, you are missing the mark of His highest and best for you, which makes you vulnerable to very tragic and traumatic things. Disobedience opens the door of your life to all the effects of the curse caused by Adam and Eve's sin. However, when you walk in obedience to God's Word, you have His power to rise above it all.

Stupidity Is Another Major Cause for Bad Things Happening in Our Lives

In our fourth lesson, we meticulously unpacked the law of sowing and reaping, which is found in Galatians 6:7. Here, Paul wrote: "Be not deceived; God is not mocked: for whatsoever a man soweth, that shall he also reap." The word "whatsoever" means *anything at all*. So this passage tells us that everything we do is a seed and that every action and every attitude, no matter what it is — good or bad — will produce a harvest.

If you sow bad seeds by doing foolish things, you are going to reap a harvest of bad things in your life, and they will be things you really will not enjoy. To reap a harvest of good things, you must continually plant good seed. This law of sowing and reaping always works, whether a person is saved or unsaved.

Galatians 6:8 goes on to say, "For he that soweth to his flesh shall of the flesh reap corruption...." We learned that the word "sow" is a continuous action. Hence, when we *sow and sow and sow* into our flesh, "...of the flesh [realm we will] reap corruption...." In the original Greek, this literally means if you plant wrong actions into your flesh, you're going to reap a lot of really bad situations in your life.

Thankfully, the opposite is also true. The Bible says, "...But he that soweth to the Spirit shall of the Spirit reap life everlasting" (Galatians 6:8). This means when you continuously sow into the things of the Spirit of God and His Kingdom, you will reap a wonderful harvest of abundant life directly out of the realm of the Spirit. Kindness, forgiveness, love, and mercy are all examples of sowing positive, good seed into the realm of the Spirit, and they will produce *an immeasurable, abundant life of positive things.*

Satan Is a Master at Creating Hindrances

Now as you have gone through these lessons, you may have wondered, *Well, what about the devil? Isn't he the cause of the problems in my life?* Yes, the devil is behind certain things that happen, which we will see clearly in a moment. But out of all the reasons for any problems we might have, the devil is the least of our worries. What most often opens the door to the painful, unwanted problems in our lives are: the curse working in the earth, a lack of knowledge, disobedience, and our own stupidity. If we can get a handle on these areas, recognizing and dealing with the devil is not as difficult as he would like you to believe. We *have* been given authority over him, so don't magnify the devil — minimize him. Exercise your authority over him in those situations and move on.

All that said, the devil is a formidable foe, and from time to time he and his minions do attack. The apostle Paul referred to this in First Thessalonians 2:17 and 18 where he wrote:

But we, brethren, being taken from you for a short time in presence, not in heart, endeavoured the more abundantly to see your face with great desire. Wherefore we would have come unto you, even I Paul, once and again; but Satan hindered us.

In this passage, we see that Paul and his team "endeavored the more abundantly" and attempted "once and again," to see the believers at Thessalonica, which means they repeatedly tried their best to see them. But Satan hindered them.

Here, Paul uses the name "Satan" — the Greek word *satanas*, which means *one who hates*, *accuses*, *slanders*, *or conspires against*. Hence, in the very name of Satan, we see the idea of a *conspiracy*. It is amazing how he works to create crazy situations to try to slow us down and stop us. That is what Paul is alluding to in this passage.

Essentially, Paul said, "We were on our way to see you, and it was really our intention to get there. But unthinkable things began to happen. Consequently, we really did our best to get to you. In fact, even I, Paul, tried again and again. But Satan, the one who creates conspiracies and makes a mess out of everything, hindered us."

The word "hindered" here is the Greek word *egkopto*, which means *to cut in on* or *to elbow out of the way*. Interestingly, this word *egkopto* was used to describe a runner who was in a race and had a fellow competitor come up alongside him and use his elbows to knock him off course and out of the race. Paul's use of this word is the equivalent of him saying, "Satan did his best to elbow us out of our position and out of the race."

Now, this word *egkopto* — translated here as "hindered" — was also used in the ancient world to describe *blocking a road* and *creating an impasse*. During that time, travelers would sometimes suddenly run into a blockage of some kind that was so severe they wouldn't be able to continue in the direction they were going. The impasse or disruption would make them have to back up and find another route to get where they needed to go.

Considering this meaning, it is as if Paul was telling the believers in Thessalonica, "We were on our way to see you, but Satan repeatedly created a blockage that we couldn't get around. We backed up and tried to take other routes, but again and again, the enemy crafted a disruption that blocked our way from getting to you."

Rick Knows Firsthand How the Enemy Creates Conspiracies

In the program, Rick shared that something unthinkable happened to him the day the construction workers were to begin working on the foundation for the ministry studio building in Moscow. Although he didn't give all the details, he said the circumstances were so bizarre and unimaginable that only Satan could have come up with such a scheme.

As the cement trucks were in position and the workers were about to begin pouring the concrete for the foundation for the TV studio, Rick got a phone call about something really outrageous that happened, and naturally speaking, it would have stopped the forward progress of the building. In that moment, he had to decide, "Am I going to give in to this fearful situation and let the devil hinder us? Or am I going to press through the opposition and keep moving ahead with the project?"

All of us will face moments like this when the devil tries to hinder us by creating an impasse or a disruption that blocks our way. And if that doesn't work, he may even attempt to cut in on us and elbow us out of the way. In Rick's case, he knew in his heart that he was in the will of God and that from the studio they were building, they were going to broadcast the trusted teaching of the Bible to the ends of the earth. So, he made the decision to stand against the enemy's attacks and knock him out of the way.

You too have the supernatural ability to knock the devil out of the way and move forward in the divine plans God has called you to do! You have been given all authority and power in the mighty name of Jesus to overthrow the enemy's efforts and trample him and his demons under your feet (*see* Luke 10:19).

Even Jesus Dealt With Satan's Attempts To Block Him From God's Will

Mark's gospel records an account of how Satan tried to block Jesus from accomplishing the Father's will in the country of the Gadarenes. Jesus and His disciples had just finished a long day of ministry and were in a boat heading across the Sea of Galilee when suddenly, "…There arose a great storm of wind, and the waves beat into the ship, so that it was now full" (Mark 4:37).

Notice the word "arose." It is the Greek word *ginomai*, which means *suddenly, out of nowhere*. In other words, this great storm of wind was the last thing the disciples would have expected, and it took them by surprise.

Interestingly, the Bible says it was a storm of "wind," which in Greek describes *turbulence*. Although they couldn't locate the source of the turbulence, they could certainly feel its effects. This monumental windstorm was manufactured by the devil to create an impasse that would keep Jesus and His men from making a great breakthrough.

The devil knew if Jesus arrived at the other side of the lake, a great miracle would take place. A demon-possessed man was going to be set free, and through his deliverance, the whole region was going to be transformed. So, out of nowhere, Satan stirred up a windstorm, which was the last thing the disciples — many of whom were seasoned fisherman — would have anticipated that night.

But Satan's moment of attack was Jesus' moment of victory. Instead of Jesus saying, "Oh no! What are we going to do?," the Bible says He rebuked the wind and spoke peace to the sea (*see* Mark 4:39). He took authority over the situation, which is exactly what we must do when the devil tries to attack us. Christ has given us all the authority and power we need to effectively deal with the devil.

A Position of Submission to God Empowers Us To Resist the Devil

Under the inspiration and unction of the Holy Spirit, James, the half-brother of Jesus wrote:

> **Submit yourselves therefore to God. Resist the devil, and he will flee from you.**
>
> —James 4:7

Now when most people quote this verse, they immediately jump to the part that says, "…Resist the devil, and he will flee from you." But before we can resist the devil, we must first submit to God. To be effective against the enemy, we must be properly aligned with the Lord. *Only when we're in a position of submission do we have the power and authority to resist the devil.*

Taking a closer look at the word "submit," we see it is the Greek word *hupotasso*, a compound of *hupo* and *tasso*. The preposition *hupo* means *under*, and the word *tasso* means *to arrange*. As a compound, the word *hupotasso* means *to properly arrange under*. It is a military term depicting a soldier's obedience and submission to authority.

In James 4:7, it signifies *one who properly arranges himself under the authority of God and His Word*. Most importantly, it pictures one who is submitted to authority as being under the covering and protection of a greater authority and who actually hides behind the authority of the one to whom he is submitted. This is amazing because this tells us that there is protection in submission.

When You 'Resist' the Devil He Will 'Flee'

In a position of submission, you have God's divine protection and the ability to resist the devil. The word "resist" in Greek is *anthistemi*, a compound of *anti* and *histemi*. The word *anti* means *against*, and the word *histemi* means *to stand*. When compounded, the word *anthistemi* means *to stand against or to stand in opposition*. It demonstrates the attitude of *one who is fiercely opposed to something and therefore determines to do everything in his power to resist it*.

Furthermore, *anthistemi* means *to defy, to stand against*, or *to withstand*, and it depicts *a well-thought-out and well-planned resistance*. This word was used in ancient Greece to picture the fierce resistance of an enemy, which again signifies that when you're properly aligned under the authority of God and hiding behind Him, He is your fierce Protecter that stands against the devil with you.

The Word of God says that when you resist the devil, he will flee (*see* James 4:7). The word "devil" — the Greek word *diabolos* — portrays *one who is known to slander, accuse, or assault* or *one who tries to ensnare others in some kind of a net or trap*. And the word "flee" is the amazing Greek word *pheugo*, which means *to flee, to take flight, to run away, to run as fast as possible*, or *to escape*. It pictures a person's feet running as fast as they can as he runs from a situation.

This word *pheugo* was used to depict a lawbreaker who flees in terror from a city or a nation where he broke the law. By using this term in this verse, James states that when you submit to God and align yourself under His authority, you are empowered to successfully resist the devil and anything he brings against you. When you are in that consecrated position of submission, the devil will "flee" from you like a criminal who flees in terror after breaking the law.

When we include the original Greek meaning of all these words, the *Renner Interpretive Version* (*RIV*) of James 4:7 is:

> **It is imperative that you make the decision to properly align yourselves under the authority of God — in a submitted position that actually provides you with protection. Being submitted to His authority gives you the ability to defy, oppose, stand steadfastly against, and withstand the accusing, slanderous, trap-setting behavior of the devil. In fact, he'll be so terrified of you that he'll move his feet as fast as he can to get away from you. Not only will he flee from you, he'll run like a criminal terrified of prosecution — so scared that he'll want to do all he can to put as much space between him and you as possible.**

Friend, that's the kind of authority you have against the enemy when you are properly submitted to the authority of God. You are so protected and so empowered you have the ability to put the devil on the run!

So if you are experiencing adverse circumstances in your life and you have eliminated the first four possible reasons and concluded it must be an attack from the devil — don't give up and throw in the towel. Instead, stay in submission to God, pray, and grab hold of the Holy Spirit's strength to stand tenaciously against the enemy. If you will make the decision not to budge and refuse to faint in the day of adversity, God will cause you to be more than a conqueror!

STUDY QUESTIONS

> Study to shew thyself approved unto God, a workman that needeth not to be ashamed, rightly dividing the word of truth.
> — 2 Timothy 2:15

1. When it comes to your spiritual authority over the enemy, do you know what God has given you? Read and write down these amazing promises from God's Word in a few different Bible translations and commit to memory the version that really grabs your attention.

- Luke 10:19 and Psalm 91:13
- Matthew 16:19 and 18:18,19
- 1 John 4:4
- Revelation 12:10,11

2. Take some time to meditate on the original Greek meaning of James 4:7, including the *Renner Interpretive Version* (*RIV*) of that verse. What new insight is the Holy Spirit showing you about how to effectively stand against the devil's attacks? What can you take from this lesson to help you stay submitted to God, resist the devil, and see him flee from you in terror?

PRACTICAL APPLICATION

> But be ye doers of the word, and not hearers only,
> deceiving your own selves.
> — James 1:22

1. Jesus and His disciples were called by God to bring deliverance to the demon-possessed man in the Gadarenes, but they were hindered by an attack from the devil in the form of a turbulent storm. Have you ever been on assignment trying to do God's will and then suddenly experienced a disruption that hindered you? If so, briefly describe what happened.
2. Ultimately, how did you handle the enemy's attack? In hindsight, can you now see the breakthrough you received that he was trying to prevent? If so, what was it? What else did you learn from that situation?
3. To effectively operate in God's authority and power and resist the enemy, you must be in a position of submission to God's authority, which includes submitting to the leaders He's placed over you. Be honest with God and yourself: Are you living in submission to God's Word and His authority? Or is there a certain area of your life where you are in disobedience to Him? Remember that there is protection in submission. If the Holy Spirit shows you something, repent and ask God to forgive you, and ask Him to help you stay in a position of submission to Him.

A Prayer To Receive Salvation

If you've never received Jesus as your Savior and Lord, now is the time for you to experience the new life Jesus wants to give you! To receive God's gift of salvation that can be obtained through Jesus alone, pray this prayer from your heart:

> *Jesus, I repent of my sin and receive You as my Savior and Lord. Wash away my sin with Your precious blood and make me completely new. I thank You that my sin is removed, and Satan no longer has any right to lay claim on me. Through Your empowering grace, I faithfully promise that I will serve You as my Lord for the rest of my life.*

If you just prayed this prayer of salvation, you are born again! You are a brand-new creation in Christ! Would you please let us know of your decision by going to **renner.org/salvation**? We would love to connect with you and pray for you as you begin your new life in Christ.

Scriptures for further study: John 3:16; John 14:6; Acts 4:12; Ephesians 1:7; Hebrews 10:19,20; 1 Peter 1:18,19; Romans 10:9,10; Colossians 1:13; 2 Corinthians 5:17; Romans 6:4; 1 Peter 1:3

CLAIM YOUR FREE RESOURCE!

As a way of introducing you further to the teaching ministry of Rick Renner, we would like to send you FREE of charge his teaching, "How To Receive a Miraculous Touch From God" on CD or as an MP3 download.

In His earthly ministry, Jesus commonly healed *all* who were sick of *all* their diseases. In this profound message, learn about the manifold dimensions of Christ's wisdom, goodness, power, and love toward all humanity who came to Him in faith with their needs.

☑ YES, I want to receive Rick Renner's monthly teaching letter!

Simply scan the QR code to claim this resource or go to:
renner.org/claim-your-free-offer

WITH US!

🏠 renner.org

facebook.com/rickrenner • facebook.com/rennerdenise
youtube.com/rennerministries • youtube.com/deniserenner
instagram.com/rickrenner • instagram.com/rennerministries_
instagram.com/rennerdenise

www.ingramcontent.com/pod-product-compliance
Lightning Source LLC
Chambersburg PA
CBHW071640040426
42452CB00009B/1703